Math = Fun!™

Count by Tens

by Jerry Pallotta
Illustrated by Rob Bolster

SCHOLASTIC INC.

New York   Toronto   London   Auckland   Sydney
Mexico City   New Delhi   Hong Kong   Buenos Aires

To Tricia, Rere, Sheila, Lizzie, Phyllis, and Eleanor!
—Jerry Pallotta

To Charlie!
—Rob Bolster

ISBN-13: 978-0-545-07068-3
ISBN-10: 0-545-07068-6

12 11 10 9 8   16 17/0

Printed in the U.S.A.   40
First printing, October 2008

We are on our way to ONE HUNDRED!
How can we get there? We are going to count by TENS.
First, let's count from one to ten, one piece of fruit at a time.
We are now at the number ONE.
This helicopter carries one strawberry.

2 two

Here we are at the number TWO.
This boat will take these two pineapples across the water.
As you count, think of different ways to travel.

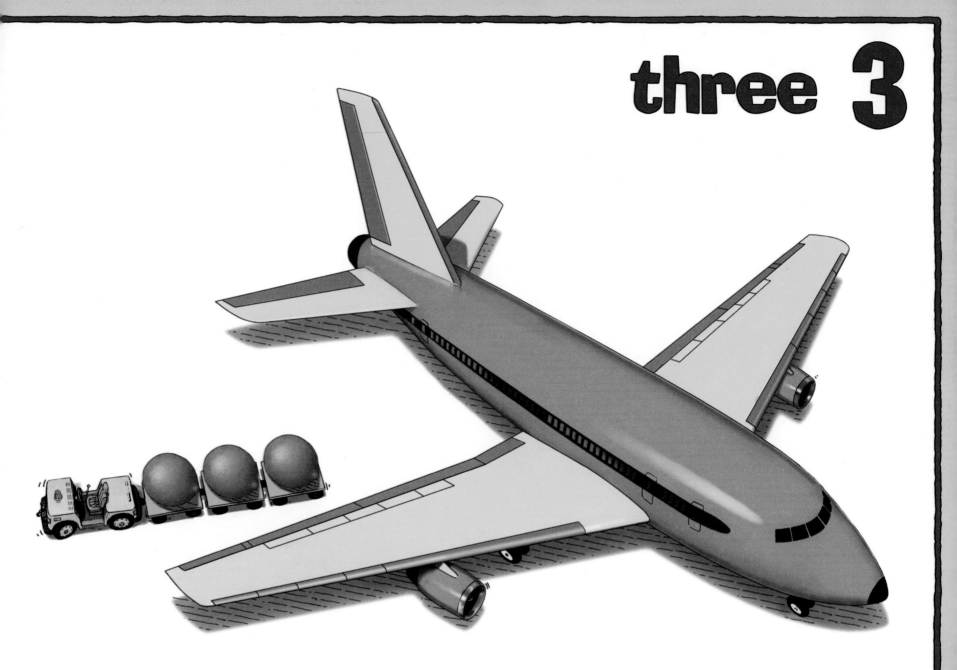

The next number on our way to ten is THREE.
Three limes are being loaded onto this jet.
Hop aboard!

4 four

Climb into the buggy and count.
One, two, three, FOUR red apples.
There are four wheels on the buggy. How many legs does a horse have?

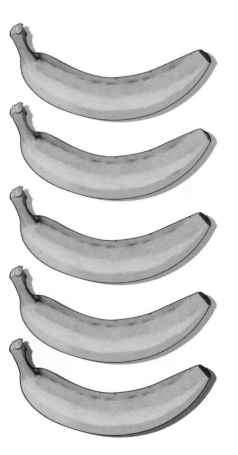

Now let's go up, up, and away in this hot air balloon.
Float with the FIVE bananas.

6 six

Beep! Beep! It's time for school. Don't miss the bus!
Look at the six peaches and count.
One, two, three, four, five, SIX!

This is your chance to fly in a blimp.
Count the SEVEN slices of watermelon.
Then grab the controls and let's fly.

8 eight

All aboard! All aboard! Get your tickets!
The train is leaving the station.
One, two, three, four, five, six, seven, EIGHT! The raspberries look yummy.

Now we are at the number NINE!
Start pedaling the bicycle. Don't stop until you get to the number ten!
Don't run over the nine blueberries.

10 ten

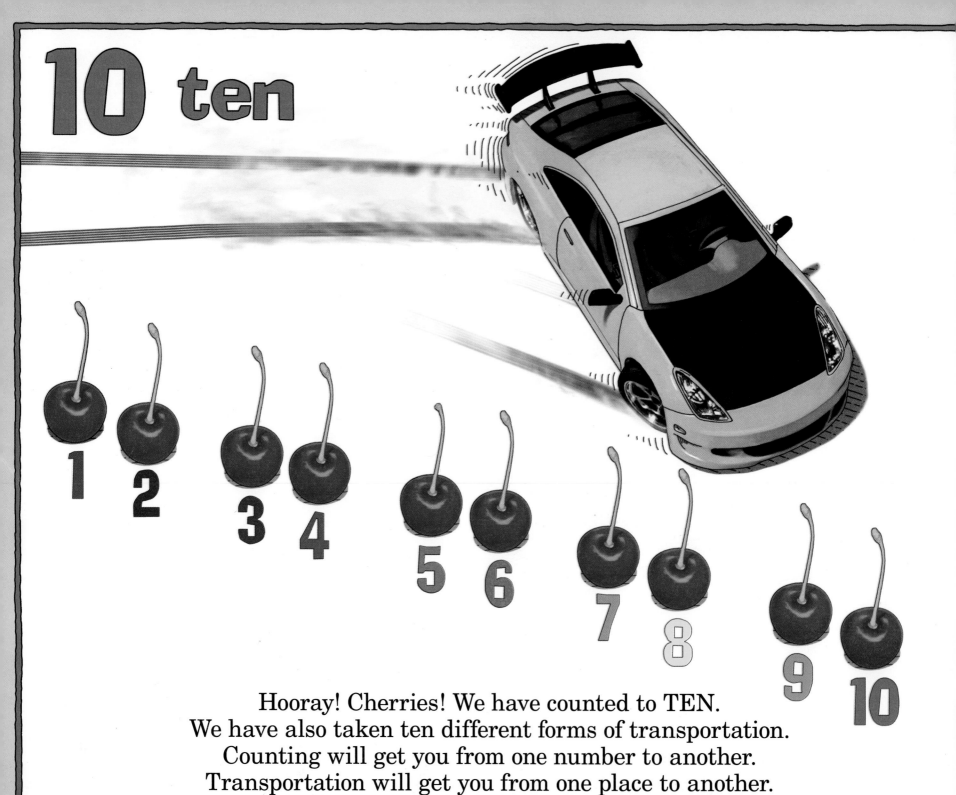

1 2 3 4 5 6 7 8 9 10

Hooray! Cherries! We have counted to TEN.
We have also taken ten different forms of transportation.
Counting will get you from one number to another.
Transportation will get you from one place to another.

ten 10

Put the sports car in reverse!
Do a review. Count again! This time, use Mt. Rainier cherries.
One, two, three, four, five, six, seven, eight, nine, TEN! We made one group of ten.
Oops! Reverse! Ten, nine, eight, seven, six, five, four, three, two, one.

20 twenty

Now we are going to count to one hundred by tens.

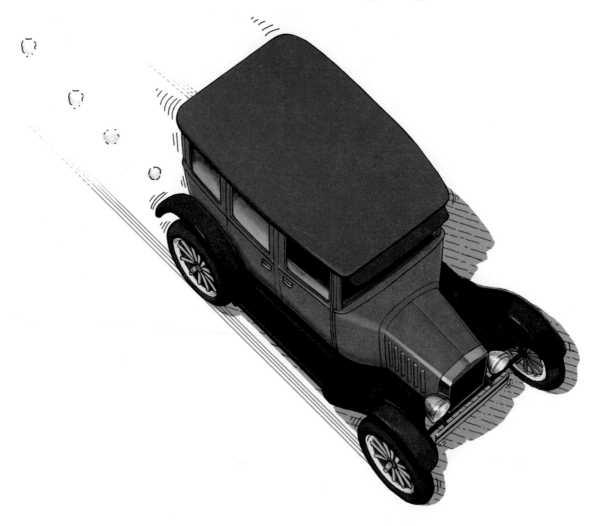

When counting by tens, the next number is not eleven.
This old Model T will take us to TWENTY!

Put the orange slices in groups of ten. Count each group by tens.

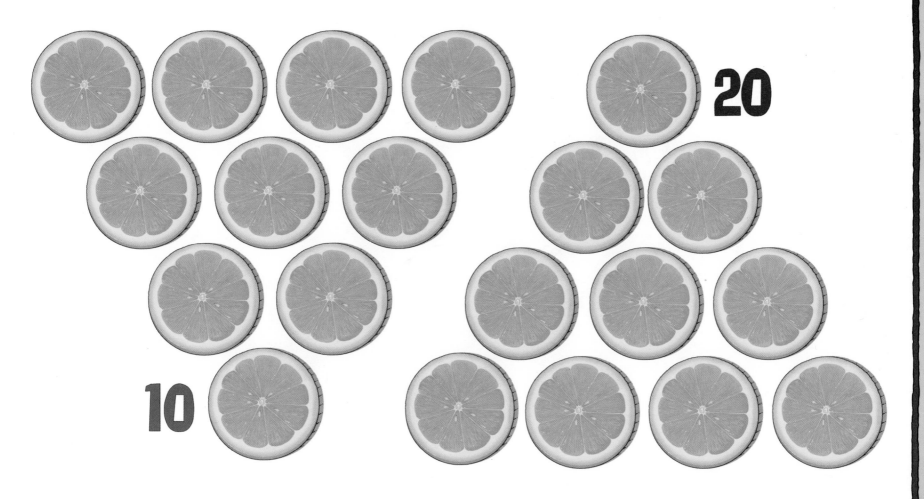

Ten, TWENTY!
Grouping makes counting easier.

30 thirty

A golf cart is another way to get around.
Wait – this is no time for sports!
We are learning to count by tens.

Grouping these cantaloupe halves by tens makes sense.

10   20   30

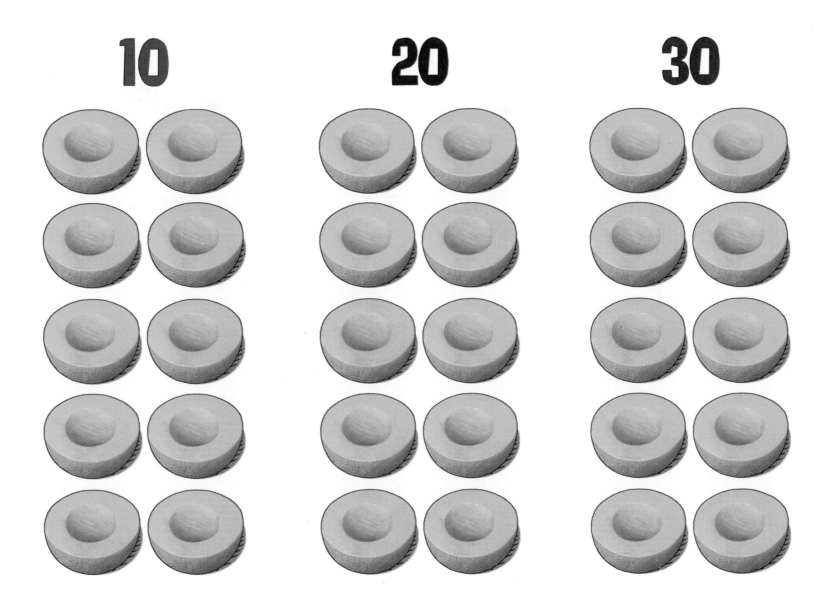

It is simple!
One, two, three. Ten, twenty, THIRTY!

40 forty

Zoom in low and count to FORTY!

Flying in a biplane is faster than walking.
Counting by tens is faster than counting by ones.

Ten, twenty, thirty, FORTY!

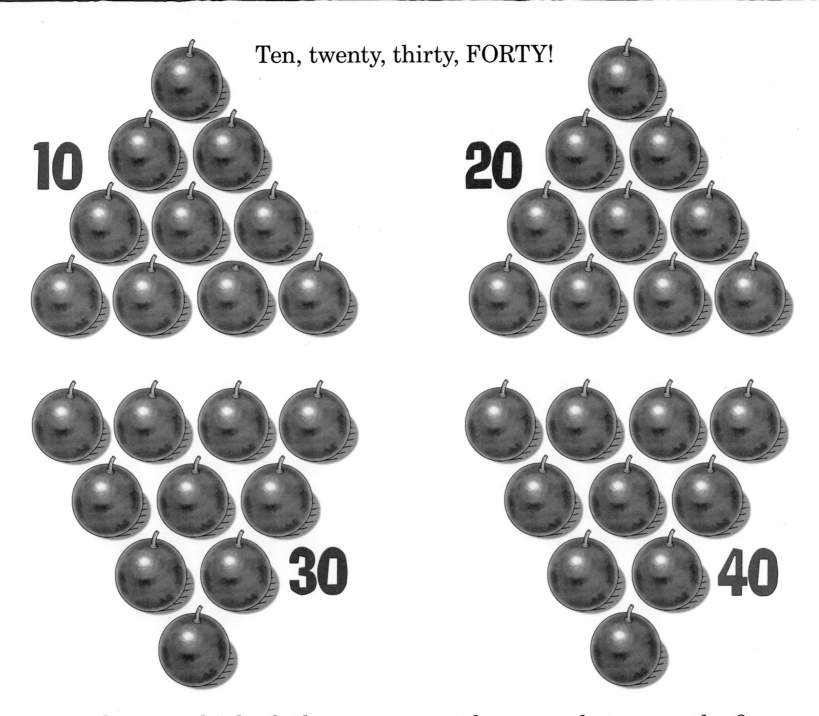

10 **20** **30** **40**

Can you think of other ways to get from one place to another?
These forty Concord grapes will make great grape juice.

50 fifty

Let's celebrate and take a cruise.

FIFTY! We are halfway to one hundred.
It's easy as one, two, three, four, five.

Ten, twenty, thirty, forty, FIFTY!

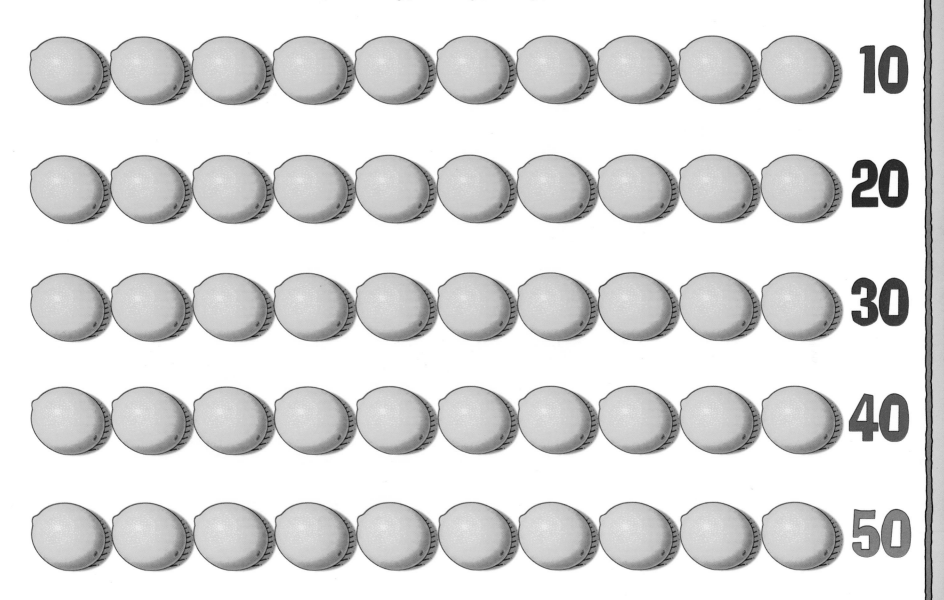

We already made groups shaped like circles, rectangles, and triangles.
Here are groups of lemons in five straight lines.
The shape of each group does not matter.
The number of pieces in each group is what is important.

60 sixty

Taxi! Taxi!
Take us to the next number.

Hop in back. Relax! Let someone else do the driving.
But please keep on counting.

Each of these six groups is made up of kiwi slices.

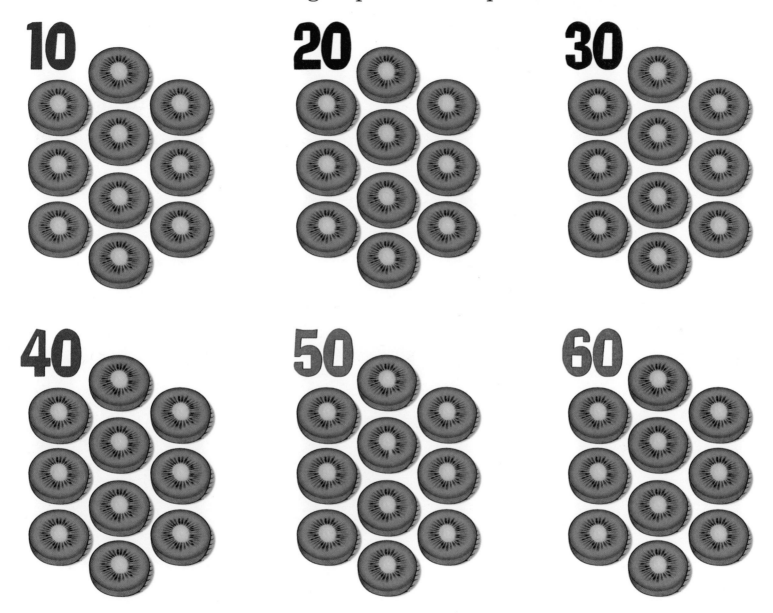

We are counting green fruit here. But the color does not matter.
Remember, the number of pieces in each group is what is important.
Ten, twenty, thirty, forty, fifty, SIXTY!

70 seventy

And now for some monster tires!

A pickup truck is another way to travel.
Motor yourself to the number SEVENTY.

Never give up! Keep on going, keep on counting.

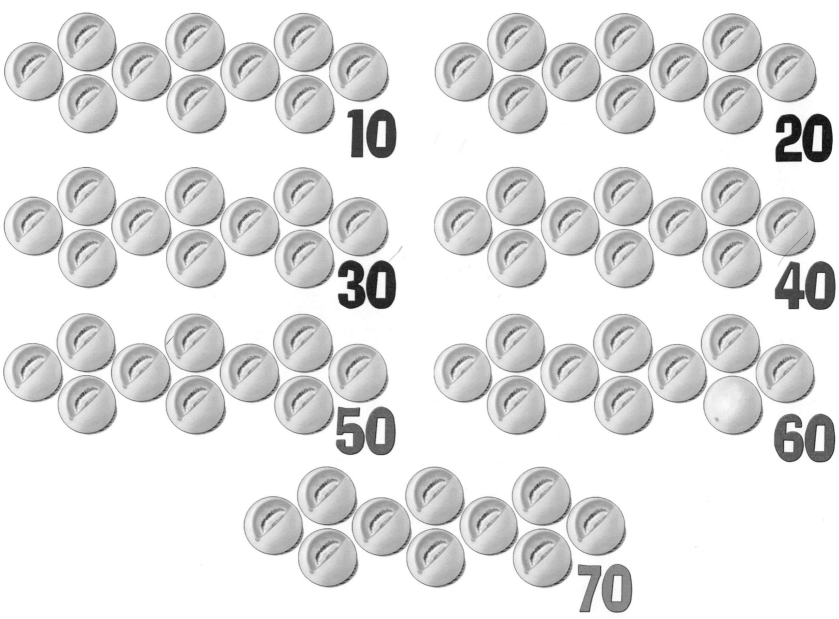

10

20

30

40

50

60

70

Ten, twenty, thirty, forty, fifty, sixty, SEVENTY!
Here are seven groups of honeydew melons.
You could also say there are seven sets.

80 eighty

Put on your space suit!
Take the space shuttle to EIGHTY!

We are on a mission – counting by tens to one hundred!

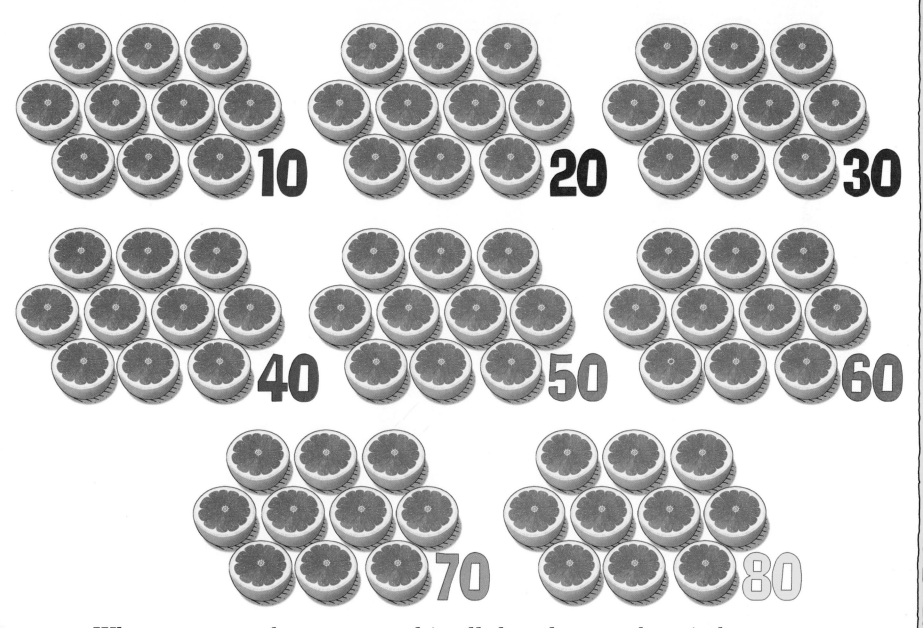

When you count by tens, you skip all the other numbers in between.
Think of other ways to count these grapefruits.
We could make groups of two, groups of four, groups of five, or groups of eight.
Nana probably sent these grapefruits from Florida.

90 ninety

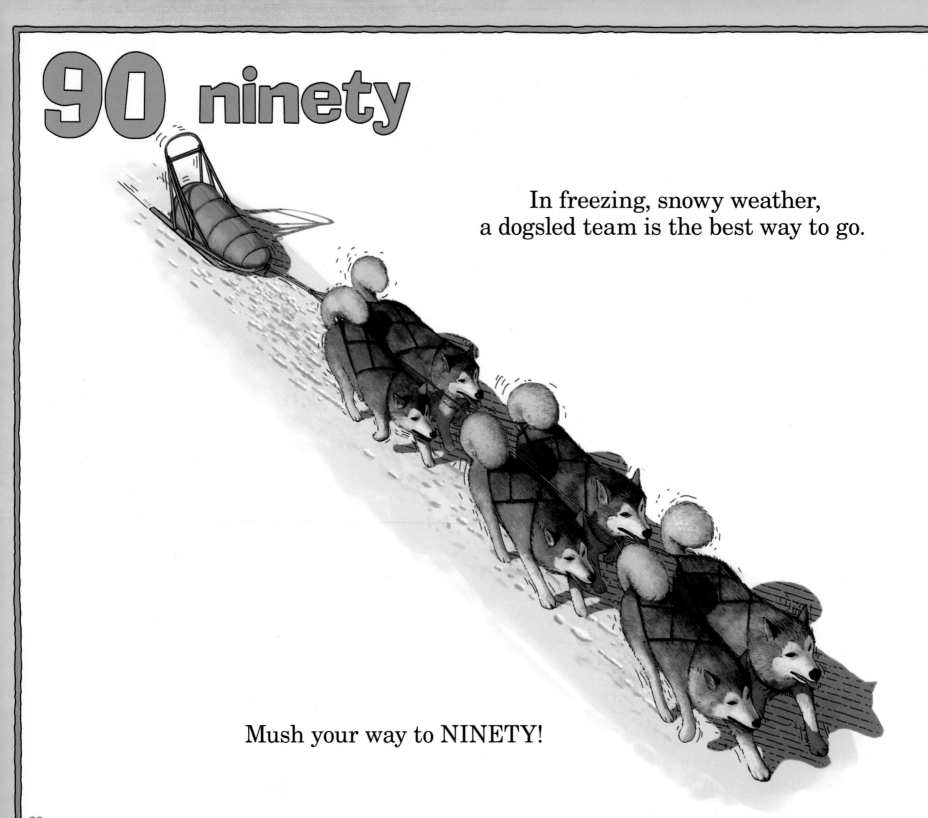

In freezing, snowy weather,
a dogsled team is the best way to go.

Mush your way to NINETY!

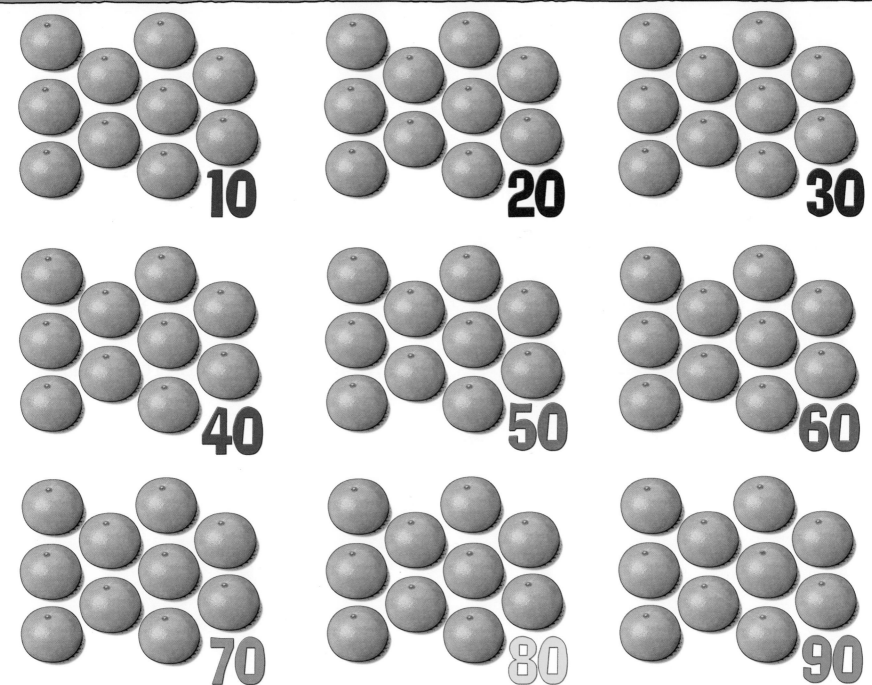

Count out tangerines to make nine groups of ten each.
One, two, three, four, five, six, seven, eight, nine, ten. Now we are at NINETY!
Only ten more pieces of fruit in a group, and we will get to one hundred.

100 one hundred

We made it to ONE HUNDRED!

Counting by tens helped us reach one hundred really quickly.
It was as if we were speeding in a dragster.

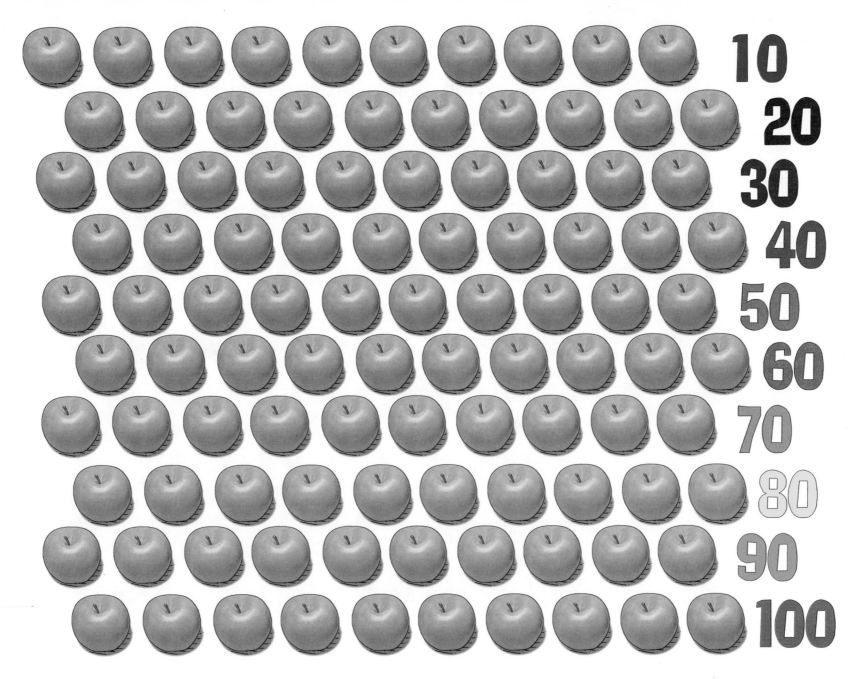

Rev up your engines. While the tires are screeching, practice!
Ten, twenty, thirty, forty, fifty, sixty, seventy, eighty, ninety, ONE HUNDRED!
We used groups of ten to count to one hundred.
Grouping and counting apples by tens makes math fun!

Hop on this unicycle and count by tens again. This time do it backward.

100 90 80 70 60 50 40 30 20 10 0

One hundred, ninety, eighty, seventy, sixty, fifty, forty, thirty, twenty, ten, ZERO! There are zero people on this page!